D1010951

RAID *on the*
INARTICULATE

RAID *on the* INARTICULATE

Poems by Deepak Chopra

IP

Infinite Possibilities Publishing

Sudbury, Massachusetts

©1996 Deepak Chopra

Published by Infinite Possibilities Products, LLC.

Editorial production: Mallika Chopra

Coordinator: Diana Cantú

Production: Deepak Singh

Design and typography: Martin St.-Martin

Cover design: Martin St.-Martin

Cover art: David Cicconi

All rights reserved. This book may not be reproduced in whole or in part, or transmitted in any form, or by any means electronic, mechanical, photocopying, recording, or other, without written permission from the publisher, except by a reviewer who may quote brief passages in a review.

ISBN 1-882971-16-7

First printing 1996
Printed in the USA on recycled paper.

Distributed by Infinite Possibilities Products, LLC.
60 Union Avenue, Sudbury, MA 01776 USA
800-858-1808 • 508-440-8400

Table of contents

Acknowledgements

I would like to express my love and gratitude to the following people for making this project a reality:

All my staff at Infinite Possibilities International in New York, Massachusetts and California. Your vision and enthusiasm is an inspiration to me.

Mallika Chopra, Deepak Singh, Diana Cantú, Martin Saint-Martin, David Cicconi, Ron Richard, and Richard Perl—the team who transformed my poems into the beautiful book you hold in your hands. I look forward to our next Infinite Possibilities publishing venture.

Special thanks to Mary Jane Sullivan for her help in editing the poetry.

Foreword

Ever since I was a child I was drawn to poetry. My grandmother would recite to me sacred verses from the mythic traditions of India where gods and goddesses frolicked in celestial playgrounds. Mystery, magic, wonder and enchantment expressed in verse became the raw materials of my imagination. Later in my childhood I was introduced to the poems of Kabir, Rumi, and Tagore who through rhythm and rhyme brought to me a sacred world that I knew existed and was real, and yet beyond my reach in the world of everyday reality. It was, nonetheless, a world that my soul yearned for...the agony of wishing and not finding.

As I grew up I came across the poems of Emily Dickinson, D. H. Lawrence, Byron, Shelley, Coleridge, Blake, Shakespeare, Chaucer and Alfred, Lord Tennyson. I began to understand the meaning and effect of onomatopoeia, where the sound echoes the sense and where just the recitation of songs, ballads and poems can lift you out of everyday existence, transporting you to higher states of awareness.

Even today, if I close my eyes to hear the exquisite verse of Tennyson's "Idylls of the King" I can see on the screen of my consciousness and hear through the stereophonic sound system of my imagination...the

1

clash of armies on the Isle of Avalon. I can sense the crunch of ice as the armored heels of King Arthur and his brave, wounded knights trudge across the snowy fields of England.

Look at the following words and see for yourself how your physiology reacts to the nostalgia of a bygone era.

Dry clashed his harness in the icy caves,
and the bare black cliff clang round him
as he based his feet on juts of slippery crag
that rang sharp, smitten with the dint of armed
heels...and on the sudden lo—the level lake and the
long glories of the winter moon.

Even now, as I read these lines I am taken inexplicably to a world that I've only experienced in the imagination, but always longed to know.

Poetry is—in the words of T.S. Eliot—a "raid on the inarticulate." This is because poetry, like mediation, allows us to slip into the gap between thoughts and get in touch with the karmic software of our souls. Here are insights and epiphanies, revelations and a world of enchantment, such as we have never dreamed of in our ordinary waking state of consciousness.

The following selection of poems is an offering from my heart. I hope that as you read them you will be inspired to sing your own song.

Author's Note

These poems are strongly influenced by some of my spiritual mentors, such as Rabindranath Tagore, Jelaluddin Rumi and others. In a few poems, I have directly borrowed a phrase or two from them.

"Ladies turning pages of poetry with indolent hands" was a sentiment expressed by W.B. Yeats in his introduction to *Gitanjali*.

"The inscrutable without name and form" was a phrase that Tagore frequently used to refer to God, as were phrases like "the lap of deathless spirit," and "the seashore of endless worlds."

In the poem *Body, mind, brain and spirit* there are two lines where I have paraphrased Robert Frost's famous expression, "We dance around the ring and suppose, While the secret sits in the middle and knows."

In the poem *We have met before* stanza four says "We have been the plantation of sugar cane, and its sweetness too." This is a direct paraphrase of a sentiment expressed by Jelaluddin Rumi.

Songs to Myself

Prisoner of words

Spells, charms, incantations
Be careful what you say...
The magic of words enfolds intention
Centuries of knowledge
Layers of experience, an entire history
In a few syllables.

Our lifetime is packaged inside us
As imprints triggered by words.
Wrapped in words the way a
Spider wraps flies in gossamer
We are both the spider and the fly
Imprisoning ourselves in our own web.

Love

Love is the spark in my heart.
Love is the light of the cosmos,
A raging flame that devours
Sun, moon and stars.
Love is the air we breathe.

It is not pleasure or even ecstasy
It is not emotion or feeling
Love is the circulation in every cell
Love is invisible and ever-present
Love is the only power.

Its universal force permeates everything
It does not possess, control or dominate
If you want love, place no conditions.

Titanic forces

I gaze upon the night sky
Looking at the flow of time
Nurturing every small step

The organization of the first hydrogen atom
The formation of stars
The birth of DNA

Out of randomness
Titanic forces swirl through the cosmos

Order, evolution, balance, intelligence
This is the force of spirit
This is the crest of the wave of life
This is the surge of love that makes me
A privileged child of the universe

I must make peace with my shadows

I am fragmented and conflicted
By so many personalities
Competing for the use of my body.
Sinners and saints are arguing
Forbidden lust and unconditional love
Divine and diabolical
The beatitude of paradise
Dark night of the soul.

Each of these have staked a claim
Shouting over each other
Causing endless trouble
Inside me saying "yes" and "no"

Guilt and shame have been implanted
and I have become stained with fear
The secret caverns and dark cells of my psyche
are riddled with doubt and shame
I have become the keeper of my shadow selves
The prisoner of my own jail
Tapping messages on the wall of my cell.

I have held on to negative energies,
Forgotten the instinct for release.
I'm a loaded battery of anger,
resentment and frustration.
I'm a bomb.
Bombs blow up and kill people.
The explosion of shrapnel is the
explosion of rage.
I must make peace with my shadows,
Bring this war to an end.

Journey to my being

I am living as a finite package of flesh and bone.
In thin wedges of space and time
I have become solid stuff
Atoms of carbon and hydrogen
and oxygen and nitrogen.
I must make a journey in the quest for alchemy
Beneath the surface of atoms and molecules
Behind the appearance of change.

I must quest beyond the boundless,
Beyond the boundaries of bone, muscle,
tissue and cell.
I must ride the crest of these clouds of energies
Beyond the play of light and shadow.
I must peel the layers of my soul
Arriving at the timeless core
At the center of my being.

Surrender

S wirling atoms of oxygen
enter my blood with every breath.

Teeming enzymes and proteins are
the tide and flood of my cells.

Electrical neuronal storms never cease.
They blast and echo in the endless
corridors of my mind.

Is this chaos another face of order?

The same tugs of gravity that created dancing stars
are holding these minuscule strands of DNA,
enfolding and unfolding the memories of
evolutionary time.

We are fooled by appearances
Uncertainty is my doorway to freedom
I have become unpredictable and odd.

continued...

Thinking, deciding, choosing and feeling
I offer these to the automatic side of my brain.

And at last, after eons of struggle and pain
I am learning to surrender to God

I am alive now.

Ticket to freedom

I have projected the same images day after day
Becoming a prisoner of the known.
But the known is dead and past now
And I must buy my ticket to freedom
By embracing the fresh unknown.

Chance encounters, unexpected coincidences
Premonitions, dreams and wishes
Flashes of unpredictable joy
Random events are
Weaving themselves in the web of time.

I have left the voice of reason.
I am listening to the beckoning whisper
In the recesses of my heart.
And new shapes of reality
Are coaxing me out of my prison.

Hidden treasures

Aware of myself
Simply as myself
In my knowingness
I embraced death
And caught her
in my arms like a lover.

In my death was my certainty of existence
Never to be born, never to cease to be,
Whatever I had lost was temporary and unreal.

When I looked in the ashes
In the rubble of devastation and disorder,
there were buried hidden treasures.

Spirit speaks

Beyond opposites of light and dark
I exist
Beyond good and evil, pleasure and pain.

Everything I see has roots in the unseen world
Nature reflects my moods
The body and mind may sleep,
I am always awake.

I possess the secret of immortality.
Living in the midst of birth and death
I pervade all the layers of reality.
Infinite worlds come and go
in the vast expanse of my consciousness.

I exist simultaneously in all times
Creating endless versions of every event
Moment by moment
I have woven the fragile threads of time
Spinning the boundless web
of eternity.

Recycled dust

This fine sand slipping through my fingers so fast
This call from the past, this quiet dust,
Is pyramids and castles and cities that did not last.
It is pharaohs, generals and beauty queens
Conspiracies, secrets and things unseen.
It is loving, passion, suffering, pain
The blood of Christ, his guts, his breath, his brain.
It is tragedy, comedy, lightning, thunder,
earthquake and storm
This raging cyclone of phenomenon and form.

Lessons of history, ancient lore
Clashing armies, death and gore
This quiet dust is the birth of stars
Titanic forces and a lonely asteroid
Elements, particles, and spiraling galaxies
in the infinite void
Queen of Sheba, Mohammed and Cleopatra
Forgiveness of God and judgment hereafter.

Laughter, crying, courage, fear
Thinking, thought, scenery, seer,
Villain and foe, hero and clown
The silent dust is everything we see
Disguising itself, it's you and me

Invisible Forces

Ageless body, timeless mind

Don't ask why,
Waves of energy bind you and me
to spring flowers and birds that fly.

To rushing brook and ocean wide
To divine beings and angels by our side.
To pre-quantum regions without dimension
From before the Fall and after the Ascension.
From before the big bang and after the universe ends
in the heat death of absolute zero.

Privileged children of the cosmos
Nothing is separate from you.
Deep inside the fabric of matter and energy
There are gods and goddesses in embryo
waiting to be born.

Flowing, flexible, dynamic, fresh
Ever-renewing, timeless, innocent,
Full of wonder, ever-guileless
Your body is the body of the universe
Uni-verse, one song.

continued...

A dizzying entry into the dance of life
Effortless, spontaneous, without struggle or strife
Where dancers disappear
If your approach is too near.
And the music fades away
Into the silence of eternity.

We join the fraternity
Where nothing is separate from you.
And deep inside the fabric
Of matter and energy
There are gods and goddesses in embryo
Waiting to be born.

You are not your atoms
They come and go
You are not your thoughts
They come and go
You are not your images
Your fierce, fearful ego
You are above and beyond these
You are the witness, the interpreter,
the self beyond all images.

You are ageless and timeless.

Body, brain, mind and spirit

Verbal cues, fed to us in early childhood,
Still run inside our heads
Like muffled tape loops.

Words, concepts, molecules, matter.
Images, symbols,
triggers for biological transformation.

Information
In form ation

Body brain mind and spirit.
Spirit, mind, body, brain
Pleasure, pain, loss, and gain
Sunshine, rain.
Are inextricably woven,
As the warp and woof
Of our lives.

continued...

Sistine Chapel, Paradise Lost
Pyramids, castles,
Palaces, monuments, Taj Mahal
You stand as mute witness to
the choreographer who invented
every step of the dance.

She was there, you never saw her.
You were not looking,
Never had a chance.

Lost in words
Images concepts
running inside your head
Like muffled tape loops
Obscure the silence
Between the notes.

The secret that sits on center stage and knows
While we dance around our lives and suppose

Body brain mind and spirit.
Spirit, mind, body, brain
Pleasure, pain, loss, and gain
Sunshine, rain.
Are inextricably woven,
As the warp and woof
Of our lives.

Creative impulses of the cosmos

The mind of God.
Where does it hide?
Creative impulses of the cosmos,
Where do you abide?

In the depths of your soul are
Boundless energies and
Powerful forces, side by side.

Infinite accomplishments with little effort.
In the eternal storehouse of creation
Are treasures beyond imagination.
Invisible forces are here to help you
They are silent outside the bounds of fear.
Step aside, do not interfere.

Look within and face the world.
In the mirror of relationships
Are secrets to be unfurled.

Wherever you go, there you are.
In this realm there is no near or far...
A speck of dirt on planet Earth
A cloud of gas on distant Mars.

A flame of candle or
Dancing light on distant stars.

There are worlds that come and go,
Like motes of dust in space and time
In this body you will not find
The me, that's free, a different kind.

In this world and not of it,
You will understand, bit by bit.
Behind the machinations of history,
Lurks a deeper mystery.

Fearless, magnificent, full of splendor.
You must enter it, naked and in surrender.

The mind of God.
Where does it hide?
Creative impulses of the cosmos,
Where do you abide?

In the depths of your soul
Are boundless energies and
Powerful forces, side by side.

Magical Beginnings

Magical beginnings

Magical beginnings and enchanted lives

The birth of stars, planet earth

Your home, your place

You come to us from the void of space

Visions of gods in the endless void

Journeying along this lonely asteroid

Darling child give us your joy

So all on earth may be healed and holy

Floating down the stream of eternity

You are becoming our destiny.
You are becoming our destiny.

I rejoice in your coming

I rejoice in your coming
Child of mine
The elements have fashioned you
Over eons of time.
Child of the universe
You are more than you seem
A wistful memory
God's dream.
Centuries of experience and desires
And yearnings have created you
Lifesongs of ages have burst into
Melodies eternally new.

I've seen in your movements
And the pulse of your heart
The dance of the cosmos
From finish to start.

The throb of your life
Coursing through my blood
Is the ebb and flow of
The tide and the flood.

Child of the universe and child of mine
I rejoice in your coming.

On the seashore of time
For a night and a day
We will meet soon and have our play.

Child of the universe
We will laugh and we will cry
But I promise you darling
We will never sigh.

You have a purpose,
A dream in your soul.
In fulfilling your dharma.
You will make life whole.

I rejoice in your coming,
Child of mine.
The elements have fashioned you
Over eons of time.

Creating a new world

Oh, ancient one
That fire can not burn
Water can not wet,
Wind can not dry,
Weapons can not cleave.

Your soul of unblemished joy,
Spirit of unbounded love,
Has danced and cascaded
And cavorted and rippled
Across the vast ocean of consciousness
And stranded on my heart and in my life.

You are supremely concentrated sweetness,
Wonder, curiosity and alertness.
You are truth, integrity, honesty and trust.
You are hope, compassion,
Peace, harmony and laughter.
You are beauty.

Courage is your essence,
Free of memories and anticipations.
The universe has conspired to create you,
Child of the universe
Child of mine.

You are the eternal
Taking birth in time.

You are the supreme being
Creating a new world.

Blissful baby

Blissful baby
who are you?
Where have you come from?

Blissful baby
you have waited patiently
since the dawn of creation.

Through turbulent tempests
and misty clouds
and violent storms
you have floated down the ages
hiding yourself in the shadows
from the womb of creation
from the lap of deathless spirit
who rules the world
the formless ocean of infinity.

You now come to this playhouse of infinite forms.

Blissful baby,
song of the cosmos
privileged child of the universe
we will love you and nurture you,
feed you, clothe you, play with you.

We are travelers together on the endless journey,
we have met for a moment
on the highway of eternity.
You are blessed and blesséd are we
the inscrutable without name and form
has brought us together.

Privileged child of the universe, let us sing our song

I know you my child

I know you my child
you are coming to us
you have been a lover so many times

A lover in life
A lover in death
A lover in the tomb
A lover from the day of resurrection
A lover in paradise
A lover forever

My love, my heart, my purest essence
you are the force that will transform this world

Agony will become ecstasy and
the secret longings of my soul
will blaze a fire
that will make us whole.

Child of the universe, you are becoming mine.

It is in the unknown that we live and move
and you, the unknown, are becoming known to me
endless versions of infinity are being precipitated
into versions of time
you are the prophet
you are the god.

My darling child,
I await your becoming from being
with bated breath.
Child of the universe,
you are becoming mine.

Sacred being

Sacred being you came as a gift from the universe.
You are made from the dust of the ground,
And spirit has breathed into you
The breath of life.
You have become a living soul.
I honor you and worship you.
All my wishes and dreams
My hopes, my aspirations, my longings
And wistful yearnings are embodied in your form

You are the infinite treasure house of formless eternity
I will love you with the force and energy of god.
You are the immeasurable potential of all
That was and is and will be
The realm of infinite possibility.

Sacred being,
Your throb of life fills me with ecstasy,
Mystery overwhelms me
When I think of your coming.

Sacred being,
You are made from the dust of the ground
And spirit has breathed into you the breath of life
So you have become a living soul
A gift from the unknown.

You are the seed of desire

Life of my life
seed of my essence
you are the seed of desire
my darling.

It was through desire that the unmanifest
made link with the manifest.
Through desire the invisible was made visible
Through desire the spirit became this body
born of dust
so wondrous to behold.

As is your desire my child,
so is your intention.
As is your intention,
so is your will.
As is your will,
so is your destiny.

You are the seed of enchanted forests
and of mystical realms
Together we will nurture our desires
in the sacred corridors of our souls
One day these desires will burst into flame
and in the burnished glow
and sudden splendor of love
we will dream a new world of reality
from the purity of our hearts.

We have met before

We have met before
perhaps you have forgotten
the tea we shared
on the bridge of rope
by the river
near the waterfall
by the mountain
in Tibet.

Or maybe it was Covent Garden,
in the England of Dickens or Yeats
while the ladies sipped champagne
turning pages of poetry
with indolent hands.

Remember those days
in those heavy mists of time?
You were father and I was child.
And so we keep reversing roles
playing out these games of life

father, son, mother, child,
lover, beloved, sinner, saint,
victor, vanquished
seer and scenery.

We have been the plantation of sugar cane,
and eaten its sweetness too.
Our destinies have been intertwined
playing out these versions, ever-new,
as we unscroll these pages of time.

I am you and you are me,
and all is one,
me and mine.

We have met before
perhaps you have forgotten
the tea we shared
on the bridge of rope
by the river
near the waterfall
by the mountain
in Tibet.

Once I was a child and did childish things

Once I was a child and did childish things
On the seashores of endless worlds I had my play,
I made and unmade my gods with worthless clay.

Once we were children and did childish things.
We carelessly frolicked on forgotten shores
dust in the dust, wind in the wind,
and though the waters were turbulent
stars and moon were mirrored in our being.

In love with life we lived the sweetest of passions,
We lived like gypsies and children of God.
Now we are grown and the wonder is gone.

Gone is the laughter, the adventure, the mystery.
My darling, my child, my teacher, my god-in-embryo
I await your manifestation with passion sublime.
Once again we will frolic on the sands of time.

The primordial one

You are the earth, wind, and fire,
You are the void of space
and the deep waters.
You are the sun, moon and dust of stars
Gestating over millennia in the crucible of creation.
you have come springing out of nothingness
bringing the entire universe with you.

You are vid, vard, word, idea and veda...
Pure knowledge, pure intelligence
Pure essence .
Divinity in motion.
You are macrocosm in microcosm
Cosmic body in human body
Cosmic mind in human mind.

Truly, you are god in embryo,
The generator, organizer
and deliverer of existence.
The total mind.

continued...

As you appear within our midst
with the sudden splendor of your magnificent being
you bring us to the sacred core of our existence
the sacrament, the covenant,
the agreement we had
that you the creator
would ever be present
and in every grain of creation.

Now I realize you were always here
and we were not looking
with eyes purified
and the mind of soul
awake once again in beams of light.

I see you in rainbows
and clouds and blades of grass
in dolphins dancing on the ocean.

In sunshine
In rain
In snows of winter
In ripened grain
In falling autumn leaves.
Omnipresent, omnipotent, omniscient.

Oh mighty one
the ancient inscrutable without name or form
Brahman, Abraham, The Primordial One.

You have come to us as this gift of child
salutations, salutations to you a million times.

You create again and again

Ever-present, all-pervading
all knowing, eternal, causeless.
Bigger than the biggest
smaller than the small
you begin your journey as
a speck of information in DNA.

Food, sound, music, image, thought,
feeling, emotion, desire, memory,
transform you into
eye, nostril, ear, brain, body
organ, cell, tissue, muscle and bone.

You are ever renewing yourself
as form and phenomenon.
Through this child
you are becoming conscious,
once again, of yourself.

Through myriad eyes,
You see yourself.

Through countless ears
you hear yourself.
Through endless mouths
You eat yourself.
Curving back within yourself
You create yourself
Again and again.

You are the slayer and the slain,
You are the creator and the creation,
The seer and the seen.

Behold this child.
From the womb of creation,
to the seed of man,
to the womb of woman,
you have come again and again,
ever dancing
your cosmic dance.

For more information on
Infinite Possibilities International

Infinite Possibilities International is the entity through which Deepak Chopra conducts his professional activities.

Infinite Possibilities offers:

- Seminars and speaking engagements in the United States and around the world, by Deepak Chopra and other leaders in the mind/body field.

- Certification programs for individuals to teach courses in meditation and mind/body/spirit health in their local communities.

- A mail order catalog which includes all books, tapes and videos by Deepak Chopra, as well as Ayurvedic herbal products.

- Media development of Deepak Chopra's ideas and works, including television, movie, public television specials and other productions.

The Global Network for Spiritual Success, the service arm of Infinite Possibilities, supports individuals committed to expanding their knowledge of human potential. The Network supports members by putting them in contact with one another for the purpose of studying and sharing questions, dreams and insights. The Global Network currently has 24,000 members from over 100 countries. Net income from the Global Network will be given to the Seven Spiritual Laws Charitable Fund, recently established at the Tides Foundation *[501(c)(3)]*.

For more information on Infinite Possibilities International and The Global Network for Spiritual Success, please contact:

Infinite Possibilities International
60 Union Avenue, Sudbury, MA, 01776 USA

(800) 858-1808 / (508) 440-8400

The Chopra Center
for Well Being

Opened in August 1996, in La Jolla, California, The Chopra Center offers panchakarma (Ayurvedic detoxification treatments), full Western and Ayurvedic medical examinations, training in yoga and meditation, special meals (with instruction in a teaching kitchen), lectures, a retail store, and the Quantum Soup cafe.

As Deepak Chopra stated, "Having written and spoken for many years on health and the human spirit, I consider the Center the heart of my life's work, dedicated to nourishing body, mind and soul." The Center team has created an environment that embodies the essence of healing, a place to explore the ocean of intelligence that lies deep within your being.

For more information on The Chopra Center for Well Being, please contact:

The Chopra Center for Well Being
7630 Fay Avenue, La Jolla, CA 92037 USA

(888) 424-6772 (toll-free) / (619) 551-7788

Printed in the U.S. on recycled paper